Lester was the son
of a son of a fisherman.
He knew Lake Michigan could be
soft as a kitten one day and
terrible as a sea monster
the next.

1

For Bill Schanen III, my first editor:
"You started a fire that will not die."
—Barbara Joosse

To Martha Fish and Diane Doering, who "showed me the ropes"
of illustration at University of Wisconsin–Extension Publications.
—Renée Graef

The author and illustrator wish to thank the Port Washington Historical Society, especially
Jackie Oleson, and also Charlie Krucky, Lloyd Smith, Kay Rego, and the Huwatschek family.

Published by the Wisconsin Historical Society Press
Publishers since 1855

The Wisconsin Historical Society helps people connect to the past by collecting, preserving, and sharing stories.
Founded in 1846, the Society is one of the nation's finest historical institutions.
Join the Wisconsin Historical Society: wisconsinhistory.org/membership

Printed in the United States of America

25 24 23 22 21   1 2 3 4 5

Library of Congress Cataloging-in-Publication Data

Names: Joosse, Barbara M., author. | Graef, Renee, illustrator.
Title: The fishermen, the horse, and the sea / Barbara Joosse & [illustrated by] Renée Graef.
Description: [Madison] : Wisconsin Historical Society Press, [2021] | Audience: Grades 2–3. |
   Summary: As the schooner "Mary Ludwig" flounders in Lake Michigan during a storm in 1895,
   fishermen on the beach send a horse, trained to haul boats in and out of the lake, to rescue the
   shipwrecked crew. Based on a true story.
Identifiers: LCCN 2021007924 (print) | LCCN 2021007925 (ebook) | ISBN 9780870209796 (hardcover) |
   ISBN 9780870209802 (epub)
Subjects: LCSH: Michigan, Lake—History—19th century—Juvenile fiction. | Wisconsin—History—19th century—
   Juvenile fiction. | CYAC: Michigan, Lake—History—19th century—Fiction. | Wisconsin—History—
   19th century—Fiction. | Fishers—Fiction. | Rescues—Fiction. | Horses—Fiction.
Classification: LCC PZ7.J7435 Fi 2021 (print) | LCC PZ7.J7435 (ebook) | DDC [E]—dc23
LC record available at https://lccn.loc.gov/2021007924
LC ebook record available at https://lccn.loc.gov/2021007925

♾ The paper used in this publication meets the minimum requirements of the American National Standard for
Information Sciences—Permanence of Paper for Printed Library Materials, ANSI Z39.48-1992.

DEATH'S DOOR

DOOR COUNTY

GREEN BAY

TRAVERSE CITY

SHEBOYGAN

LUDINGTON

PORT WASHINGTON

Sucker Brook

MUSKEGON

MILWAUKEE

The Fishermen, the Horse, and the Sea

RACINE

HOLLAND

KENOSHA

Written by Barbara Joosse
Illustrated by
Renée Graef

ST. JOSEPH

CHICAGO

MICHIGAN CITY

GARY

On sunny summer days, the lake spilled over with joy, washing to the sand with cool foamy fingers while the sun cast jewels across the water. On those days, Lester collected driftwood branches, stacking them into a tent on the sand and playing with Evelyn inside. Sometimes he waded with Mama till the water reached his waist. They never waded farther, though, and Lester never waded alone.

Evelyn wasn't allowed to go into the lake at all, even holding Mama's hand. She was too little.

On other days, the sky grew green and bruised, and the sea snarled. The gulls didn't fly, and the ducks huddled close to shore. Then Mama twisted her ring this way and that, worrying over Papa and Uncle Herbert out on the water.

On those days, Mama did the things she always did: built a toasty fire in the stove, set out dough to rise, made stew. But she never lost sight of the lake, not for one second, not till she spied their speck-of-a-boat on the water.

Then she sent for the horse owned by the Frank family down the beach—a fisherman's horse who loved the water. The big coach horse pulled the flat-bottom boat to shore, depositing the two fishermen safe and sound.

Soon Papa and Uncle Herbert filled the doorway. Lester and Evelyn rushed into big arms, pressing their noses into woolen sweaters that smelled of the men, the fish, and the sea.

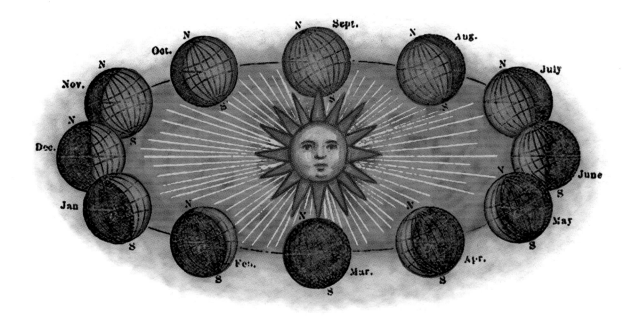

The autumn equinox of 1895 was a time when Mama worried.

On the equinox, the day is exactly as long as the night. For people who work on the land, it's a time of harvesting crops, pressing apples into cider, and gazing at the moon. But for those on the sea, it's a time of worry. They believe wicked storms are brewed when the sun crosses the equator.

That night, the wind shook the family's little house at Sucker Brook, shook it to the rafters. The roar of the breakers kept everyone awake except Lester and Evelyn. They slept soundly, knowing Papa and Uncle Herbert were safe at home.

The grown-ups huddled at the rough-scrubbed table, drinking strong coffee. Papa thought he heard voices on the lake, calling for help. But it was dark as a fish-belly outside, too dark to see. And so they waited.

At first dawn, Mama, Papa, and Uncle Herbert gathered on the beach and peered into the dim light. There! On the lake! A schooner in trouble!

The *Mary Ludwig* had lost a mast, and her sails were ripped to shreds. The crewmen had thrown out an anchor, so the boat stayed put, but it was taking on water. Mama drew in a breath. Were the men trying to escape the *Mary Ludwig* by launching a small rowboat? Into the horrible storm? They would never survive!

Mama untied her apron, and Papa fastened it to an oar. He waved it back and forth to warn the crewmen—a red signal of danger!

Inside, Lester woke with a start. Something felt wrong! He didn't hear footsteps in the kitchen or the sizzle of bacon in a frypan. Where was Mama in her red apron? Where were Uncle Herbert and Papa?

From the window, Lester spied Papa on the beach, waving the oar with its apron flag, and he knew: something terrible was happening on the lake. He wanted to see for himself! He wanted to be with them!

Lester rushed to the beach and huddled with his family as they watched the two crewmen crawl into their small rowboat. The boat rode a breaker up and up, then slid out of sight, then appeared again, impossibly small on the swell of a mountainous wave.

The crewmen were strong, but the storm was stronger. Their boat overturned, spilling them into the angry sea. Bobbing like corks, they grabbed the overturned boat—one at the front, one at the back—and held on for dear life.

Among fishermen, there's a code: We take care of our own. Papa and Uncle Herbert *had* to rescue the two men. Together, they launched their own good boat and bent their backs into the oars. But the waves beat them back, slamming their boat onto the beach again and again. If Papa and Uncle Herbert couldn't make it to the boat, the crewmen would surely drown.

A small group of fishermen gathered on the beach, knowing one of their own was in trouble. But what could they do to help? Was anyone big and strong and brave enough to plow through the waves?

Papa had an idea, and everyone agreed. The Frank horse!

Papa was a big man. Too big. He knew he would weigh down the horse. So he helped Mr. Gunther, a smaller man, onto the horse's bare, broad back.

Everyone knew the Frank horse loved the sea. But a horse can't hold its breath. If a big wave washed over the horse's head, he might drown. And these waves were big as mountains! Would the horse dare to go into the water?

But, like the fishermen he served, this horse was huge in body and in heart. When he spied the shipwrecked men, he plunged into the lake. Head high, he snorted at the breakers as if they were nothing. He swam onward with his eyes on the men who needed help.

From the beach, Lester watched one of the crewmen slip into the icy water and knew he was gone. Lester reached for Mama's hand for comfort. The horse was swimming faster now, racing for the man still clinging to the boat. At last, the Frank horse was there. The shivering man reached toward him but didn't have the strength to climb onto the horse's slippery back!

The horse knew what to do. He turned, offering his tail to the drowning crewman as a rope. Fingers numb with cold, the man held on as best he could, slipping, but never letting go. The Frank horse pulled him through wild wind and water—wave after crashing wave—until they were, at last, safely on shore.

Mama, already in the house, had everything ready. She welcomed the stranger—his lips blue with cold and his face white as death—with a warm fire, blankets, hot coffee, and rum.

And the Frank horse?
He was returned to his warm stable, rubbed down,
and treated to an extra helping of oats.

In time, Lester grew into a man,
a man with a family, a fisherman brave and strong—
just like his father and grandfather.
But he never forgot the story
of the fishermen, the horse, and the sea.

After the storm, the cargo ship ***Mary Ludwig*** was taken into
Port Washington to be pumped out. But as she was pulled
from her resting spot, the anchor's chain snapped, and
the anchor was left behind. After being pumped out and
restored, the *Mary Ludwig* resumed her life as a cargo
ship. In the 1900s, she transported a merry-go-round
to fairs along the coast of Lake Michigan.

In the early 1980s, sonar detected something just
off the cost of Port Washington, 30 or 40 feet underwater.
A diver went down to inspect and found an anchor and 25 feet of broken chain
hooked to a huge rock. Were the anchor and chain from the *Mary Ludwig*? No one ever
knew for sure.

A **schooner** (skoo-ner) is a sailing ship with two or more masts (poles that hold
the sails upright). In 1895, most schooners were cargo ships.

Lake Michigan is one of five freshwater Great Lakes of North America,
and it really is *great*! It's 307 miles long and 118 miles wide! Due to its sea-like
characteristics (rolling waves, sustained winds, strong currents, great depths, and far-
reaching horizons), Lake Michigan is sometimes called an "inland sea."

A **breaker** refers to a breaking wave—a wave that swells large, then crests
and breaks. The breakers in Lake Michigan are often more dangerous than those
in the oceans because the lake's waves are not as deep and its breakers are shorter,
choppier, and more difficult to ride. The most dangerous waves break close to shore.

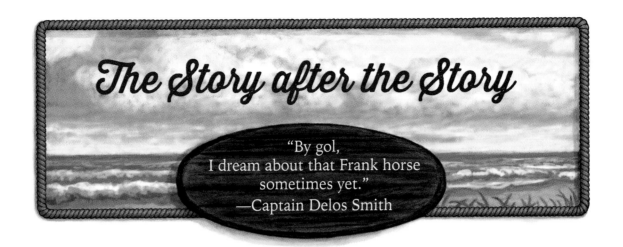

"By gol,
I dream about that Frank horse
sometimes yet."
—Captain Delos Smith

The **Frank horse,** owned by a family with the last name Frank, loved to swim. Not many horses love to swim the way the Frank horse did. In fact, many horses don't like to swim at all!

The Smith family used the Frank horse to haul boats and pile drivers in and out of the lake. There's no record of his name, and perhaps he didn't have one. In 1895, horses were often considered livestock, not pets, and they didn't always have names.

The shipwrecked crewman saved by the Frank horse was **Mr. Hogan.** News articles from the time referred to him as a "roustabout" and called him "Mr. Hogan from Everywhere," meaning he accepted jobs on a variety of ships.

Captain Delos Smith (or "Papa" to Lester) built a prosperous business with his brother, Herbert, around a fleet of commercial fishing boats. Eventually the business grew to include the Smith Bros. Fish Shanty restaurant. In the 1890s, Delos and Herbert moved their enterprise from Sucker Brook to nearby Port Washington where there were better shipping and mooring facilities. Delos assisted in two other rescues at sea: 64 passengers from the burning steamer *Atlanta* and 15 seamen from the car-carrier *Senator,* which collided with another boat, *Marquette,* in the fog. But the Frank horse rescue was closest to his heart.

Photo courtesy of the Smith & Huwatschek families

Delos Smith

For the most part, **Delia Smith** (or "Mama" to Lester) did the things many women did at that time: she cooked, mended, cleaned, and raised her family. In those days, it was generally assumed that men and women would perform different jobs. Today, men and women have the ability to choose their own professions and tasks.

Evelyn Smith was three years old in 1895 when this story took place. When she grew up, she did not let gender roles determine her life's path. Evelyn had a talent for business. She created the Smith Bros. fish sandwich, which became so popular she later developed the family's successful restaurant, the Smith Bros. Fish Shanty. She also discovered a way to turn fish oil into an inexpensive source of vitamins that helped people during the Great Depression.

In addition, she became the first industrial nurse in Milwaukee, served in a MASH (or Mobile Army Surgical Hospital) unit in France during World War I, homesteaded in Montana, became active in women's rights in Milwaukee, and founded a tuberculosis sanitarium and children's camp.

Evelyn Smith

Lester, Evelyn & Oliver

Lester Smith was five years old at the time of the Frank horse rescue. Later, he served in World War I, crossing the Atlantic 22 times on a British transport ship as the highest ranking American on board. Later, he became the head of the Smith Bros. family business. He fought for many improvements in the fishing industry and was instrumental in promoting fish conservation practices.

The **Smith Bros. Fish Shanty** was established in 1934.
The restaurant began with 3 tables and 12 counter stools.
By 1940, the restaurant had expanded to 250 seats and
had become a favorite destination for diners across the country.
By 1951, the enterprise had expanded to include three restaurants—
one in Port Washington, Wisconsin; one in Torrance, California;
and one in Los Angeles, California—
and they were all managed by Evelyn Smith.